Lead in Construction

U.S. Department of Labor

Occupational Safety and Health Administration

OSHA 3142-12R
2004

Contents

Health Hazards of Lead Exposure

Pure lead (Pb) is a heavy metal at room temperature and pressure. A basic chemical element, it can combine with various other substances to form numerous lead compounds.

Lead has been poisoning workers for thousands of years. Lead can damage the central nervous system, cardiovascular system, reproductive system, hematological system, and kidneys. When absorbed into the body in high enough doses, lead can be toxic.

In addition, workers' lead exposure can harm their children's development.

Short-term (acute) overexposure–as short as days--can cause acute encephalopathy, a condition affecting the brain that develops quickly into seizures, coma, and death from cardiorespiratory arrest. Short-term occupational exposures of this type are highly unusual but not impossible.

Extended, long-term (chronic) overexposure can result in severe damage to the central nervous system, particularly the brain. It can also damage the blood-forming, urinary, and reproductive systems. There is no sharp dividing line between rapidly developing acute effects of lead and chronic effects that take longer to develop.

SYMPTOMS OF CHRONIC OVEREXPOSURE

Some of the common symptoms include:

- Loss of appetite;
- Constipation;
- Nausea;
- Excessive tiredness;
- Headache;
- Fine tremors;
- Colic with severe abdominal pain;
- Metallic taste in the mouth;
- Weakness;
- Nervous irritability;
- Hyperactivity;

- Muscle and joint pain or soreness;
- Anxiety;
- Pallor;
- Insomnia;
- Numbness; and
- Dizziness.

REPRODUCTIVE RISKS

Lead is toxic to both male and female reproductive systems. Lead can alter the structure of sperm cells and there is evidence of miscarriage and stillbirth in women exposed to lead or whose partners have been exposed. Children born to parents who were exposed to excess lead levels are more likely to have birth defects, mental retardation, or behavioral disorders or to die during the first year of childhood.

Workers who desire medical advice about reproductive issues related to lead should contact qualified medical personnel to arrange for a job evaluation and medical followup--particularly if they are pregnant or actively seeking to have a child. Employers whose employees may be exposed to lead and who have been contacted by employees with concerns about reproductive issues must make medical examinations and consultations available.

CHELATING AGENTS

Under certain limited circumstances, a physician may prescribe special drugs called chelating agents to reduce the amount of lead absorbed in body tissues. Using chelation as a preventive measure--that is, to lower blood level but continue to expose a worker--is prohibited and therapeutic or diagnostic chelations of lead that are required must be done under the supervision of a licensed physician in a clinical setting, with thorough and appropriate medical monitoring. The employee must be notified in writing before treatment of potential consequences and allowed to obtain a second opinion.

Worker Exposure

Lead is most commonly absorbed into the body by inhalation. When workers breathe in lead as a dust, fume, or mist, their lungs and upper respiratory tract absorb it into the body. They can also absorb lead through the digestive system if it enters the mouth and is ingested.

A significant portion of the lead inhaled or ingested gets into the bloodstream. Once in the bloodstream, lead circulates through the body and is stored in various organs and body tissues. Some of this lead is filtered out of the body quickly and excreted, but some remains in the blood and tissues. As exposure continues, the amount stored will increase if the body absorbs more lead than it excretes. The lead stored in the tissue can slowly cause irreversible damage, first to individual cells, then to organs and whole body systems.

Construction Workers and Lead Exposure

HOW LEAD IS USED

In construction, lead is used frequently for roofs, cornices, tank linings, and electrical conduits. In plumbing, soft solder, used chiefly for soldering tinplate and copper pipe joints, is an alloy of lead and tin. Soft solder has been banned for many uses in the United States. In addition, the Consumer Product Safety Commission bans the use of lead-based paint in residences. Because lead-based paint inhibits the rusting and corrosion of iron and steel, however, lead continues to be used on bridges, railways, ships, lighthouses, and other steel structures, although substitute coatings are available.

Construction projects vary in their scope and potential for exposing workers to lead and other hazards. Projects such as removing paint from a few interior residential doors may involve limited exposure. Others projects, however, may involve removing or stripping substantial quantities of lead-based paints on large bridges and other structures.

MOST VULNERABLE WORKERS

Workers potentially at risk for lead exposure include those involved in iron work; demolition work; painting; lead-based paint

abatement; plumbing; heating and air conditioning maintenance and repair; electrical work; and carpentry, renovation, and remodeling work. Plumbers, welders, and painters are among those workers most exposed to lead. Significant lead exposures also can arise from removing paint from surfaces previously coated with lead-based paint such as bridges, residences being renovated, and structures being demolished or salvaged. With the increase in highway work, bridge repair, residential lead abatement, and residential remodeling, the potential for exposure to lead-based paint has become more common.

Workers at the highest risk of lead exposure are those involved in:

- Abrasive blasting and
- Welding, cutting, and burning on steel structures.

Other operations with the potential to expose workers to lead include:

- Lead burning;
- Using lead-containing mortar;
- Power tool cleaning without dust collection systems;
- Rivet busting;
- Cleanup activities where dry expendable abrasives are used;
- Movement and removal of abrasive blasting enclosures;
- Manual dry scraping and sanding;
- Manual demolition of structures;
- Heat-gun applications;
- Power tool cleaning with dust collection systems; and
- Spray painting with lead-based paint.

OSHA's Lead Standard

OSHA's Lead Standard for the Construction Industry, Title 29 Code of Federal Regulations 1926.62, covers lead in a variety of forms, including metallic lead, all inorganic lead compounds, and organic lead soaps.

EXPOSURE LIMITS

The standard establishes maximum limits of exposure to lead for all workers covered, including a permissible exposure limit (PEL) and action level (AL).

The PEL sets the maximum worker exposure to lead: 50 micrograms of lead per cubic meter of air (50μg/m3) averaged over an eight-hour period. If employees are exposed to lead for more than eight hours in a workday, their allowable exposure as a TWA for that day must be reduced according to this formula:

Employee exposure (in μg/m3) = 400 divided by the hours worked in the day.

The AL, regardless of respirator use, is an airborne concentration of 30μg/m3, averaged over an eight-hour period. The AL is the level at which an employer must begin specific compliance activities outlined in the standard.

APPLICABILITY TO CONSTRUCTION

OSHA's lead in construction standard applies to all construction work where an employee may be exposed to lead. All work related to construction, alteration, or repair, including painting and decorating, is included. Under this standard, construction includes, but is not limited to:

- Demolition or salvage of structures where lead or materials containing lead are present;
- Removal or encapsulation of materials containing lead;
- New construction, alteration, repair, or renovation of structures, substrates, or portions or materials containing lead;
- Installation of products containing lead;
- Lead contamination from emergency cleanup;
- Transportation, disposal, storage, or containment of lead or materials containing lead where construction activities are performed; and
- Maintenance operations associated with these construction activities.

Employer Responsibilities

Employers of construction workers are responsible for developing and implementing a worker protection program. At a minimum, the employer's worker protection program for employees exposed to lead above the PEL should include:

- Hazard determination, including exposure assessment;
- Medical surveillance and provisions for medical removal;
- Job-specific compliance programs;
- Engineering and work practice controls;
- Respiratory protection;
- Protective clothing and equipment;
- Housekeeping;
- Hygiene facilities and practices;
- Signs;
- Employee information and training; and
- Recordkeeping.

Because lead is a cumulative and persistent toxic substance and health effects may result from exposure over prolonged periods, employers must use these precautions where feasible to minimize employee exposure to lead.

The employer should, as needed, consult a qualified safety and health professional to develop and implement an effective, site-specific worker protection program. These professionals may work independently or may be associated with an insurance carrier, trade organization, or on-site consultation program.

For each job where employee exposure exceeds the PEL, the employer must establish and implement a written compliance program to reduce employee exposure to the PEL or below. The compliance program must provide for frequent and regular inspections of job sites, materials, and equipment by a competent person. Written programs, which must be reviewed and updated at least every six months, must include:

- A description of each activity in which lead is emitted (such as equipment used, material involved, controls in place, crew size, employee job responsibilities, operating procedures, and maintenance practices);

- The means to be used to achieve compliance and engineering plans and studies used to determine the engineering controls selected where they are required;

- Information on the technology considered to meet the PEL;

- Air monitoring data that document the source of lead emissions;

- A detailed schedule for implementing the program, including copies of documentation (such as purchase orders for equipment, construction contracts);

- A work practice program;

- An administrative control schedule, if applicable; and

- Arrangements made among contractors on multi-contractor sites to inform employees of potential lead exposure.

Hazard Assessment

An employer is required to conduct an initial employee exposure assessment of whether employees are exposed to lead at or above the AL based on:

- Any information, observation, or calculation that indicates employee exposure to lead;

- Any previous measurements of airborne lead; and

- Any employee complaints of symptoms attributable to lead exposure.

Objective data and historical measurements of lead may be used to satisfy the standard's initial monitoring requirements.

INITIAL EMPLOYEE EXPOSURE ASSESSMENT

Initial monitoring may be limited to a representative sample of those employees exposed to the greatest concentrations of airborne lead. Representative exposure sampling is permitted when there are a number of employees performing the same job, with

lead exposure of similar duration and level, under essentially the same conditions. For employees engaged in similar work, the standard requires that the members of the group reasonably expected to have the highest exposure levels be monitored. This result is then attributed to the other employees of the group.

The employer must establish and maintain an accurate record documenting the nature and relevancy of previous exposure data. Instead of performing initial monitoring, the employer may in some cases rely on objective data that demonstrate that a particular lead-containing material or product cannot result in employee exposure at or above the action level when it is processed, used, or handled.

BIOLOGICAL MONITORING TESTS

Analysis of blood lead samples must be conducted by an OSHA-approved lab and be accurate (to a confidence level of 95 percent) within plus or minus 15 percent, or 6 µg/dl, whichever is greater. If an employee's airborne lead level is at or above the AL for more than 30 days in any consecutive 12 months, the employer must make biological monitoring available on the following schedule:

- At least every two months for the first six months and every six months thereafter for employees exposed at or above the action level for more than 30 days annually;
- At least every two months for employees whose last blood sampling and analysis indicated a blood lead level at or above 40 µg/dl; and
- At least monthly while an employee is removed from exposure due an elevated blood lead level.

PENDING EMPLOYEE EXPOSURE ASSESSMENT

Until the employer performs an exposure assessment and documents that employees are not exposed above the PEL, OSHA requires some degree of interim protection for employees. This means providing respiratory protection, protective work clothing and equipment, hygiene facilities, biological monitoring, and training—as specified by the standards—for certain tasks prone to produce high exposure. These include:

- Manual demolition of structures such as dry wall, manual scraping, manual sanding, and use of a heat gun where lead-containing coatings or paints are present;
- Power tool cleaning with or without local exhaust ventilation;
- Spray painting with lead-containing paint;
- Lead burning;
- Use of lead-containing mortar;
- Abrasive blasting, rivet busting, welding, cutting, or torch-burning on any structure where lead-containing coatings or paint are present;
- Abrasive blasting enclosure movement and removal;
- Cleanup of activities where dry expendable abrasives are used; and
- Any other task the employer believes may cause exposures in excess of the PEL.

TEST RESULTS SHOWING NO OVEREXPOSURES

If the initial assessment indicates that no employee is exposed above the AL, the employer may discontinue monitoring. Further exposure testing is not required unless there is a change in processes or controls that may result in additional employees being exposed to lead at or above the AL, or may result in employees already exposed at or above the AL being exposed above the PEL. The employer must keep a written record of the determination, including the date, location within the work site, and the name and social security number of each monitored employee.

EMPLOYEE NOTIFICATION OF MONITORING RESULTS

The employer must notify each employee in writing of employee exposure assessment results within five working days of receiving them. Whenever the results indicate that the representative employee exposure, without the use of respirators, is above the PEL, the employer must include a written notice stating that the employee's exposure exceeded the PEL and describing corrective action taken or to be taken to reduce exposure to or below the PEL.

www.osha.gov

Medical Surveillance

When an employee's airborne exposure is at or above the AL for more than 30 days in any consecutive 12 months, an immediate medical consultation is required when the employee notifies the employer that he or she:

- Has developed signs or symptoms commonly associated with lead-related disease;
- Has demonstrated difficulty in breathing during respirator use or a fit test;
- Desires medical advice concerning the effects of past or current lead exposure on the employee's ability to have a healthy child; and
- Is under medical removal and has a medically appropriate need.

MEDICAL EXAMS

The best indicator of personal lead exposure is through a blood test to indicate elevated blood lead levels. A medical exam must also include:

- Detailed work and medical histories, with particular attention to past lead exposure (occupational and nonoccupational), personal habits (smoking and hygiene), and past gastro-intestinal, hematologic, renal, cardiovascular, reproductive, and neurological problems;
- A thorough physical exam, with particular attention to gums, teeth, hematologic, gastrointestinal, renal, cardiovascular, and neurological systems; evaluation of lung function if respirators are used;
- A blood pressure measurement;
- A blood sample and analysis to determine blood lead level;

    • Hemoglobin and hematocrit determinations, red cell indices, and an exam of peripheral smear morphology; and

    • Zinc protopor-phyrin; blood urea nitrogen; and serum creatinine;
- A routine urinalysis with microscopic exam; and
- Any lab or other test the examining physician deems necessary.

INFORMATION FOR THE EXAMINING PHYSICIAN

The employer must provide all examining physicians with a copy of the lead in construction standard, including all appendices, a description of the affected employee's duties as they relate to the employee's exposure, the employee's lead exposure level or antici-pated exposure level, a description of personal protective equipment used or to be used, prior blood lead determinations, and all prior written medical opinions for the employee.

WHEN MONITORING SHOWS EMPLOYEE EXPOSURES ABOVE THE AL

Employers must make available, at no cost to the employee, initial medical surveillance for employees exposed to lead on the job at or above the action level on any one day per year. This initial medical surveillance consists of biological monitoring in the form of blood sampling and analysis for lead and zinc protoporyrin (ZPP) levels. In addition, a medical surveillance program with biological monitoring must be made available to any employee exposed at or above the action level for more than 30 days in any consecutive 12 months.

AFTER THE MEDICAL EXAMINATION

Employers must obtain and provide the employee a copy of a written opinion from each examining or consulting physician that contains only information related to occupational exposure to lead and must include:

- Whether the employee has any detected medical condition that would increase the health risk from lead exposure;
- Any special protective measures or limitations on the worker's exposure to lead,
- Any limitation on respirator use; and
- Results of the blood lead determinations.

In addition, the written statement may include a statement that the physician has informed the employee of the results of the con-sultation or medical examination and any medical condition that may require further examination or treatment.

The employer must instruct the physician that findings, including lab results or diagnoses unrelated to the worker's lead exposure, must not be revealed to the employer or included in the written opinion to the employer. The employer must also instruct the physician to advise employees of any medical condition, occupational or non-occupational, that necessitates further evaluation or treatment. In addition, some states also require laboratories and health care providers to report cases of elevated blood lead concentrations to their state health departments.

Medical Removal Provisions

Temporary medical removal can result from an elevated blood level or a written medical opinion. More specifically, the employer is required to remove from work an employee with a lead exposure at or above the AL each time periodic and follow-up (within two weeks of the periodic test) blood sampling tests indicate that the employee's blood level is at or above 50 µg /dl. The employer also must remove from work an employee with lead exposure at or above the AL each time a final medical determination indicates that the employee needs reduced lead exposure for medical reasons. If the physician who is implementing the employer's medical program makes a final written opinion recommending the employee's removal or other special protective measures, the employer must implement the physician's recommendation.

For an employee removed from exposure to lead at or above the AL due to a blood lead level at or above 50 µg/dl, the employer may return that employee to former job status when two consecutive blood sampling tests indicate that the employee's blood lead level is below 40 µg /dl. For an employee removed from exposure to lead due to a final medical determination, the employee must be returned when a subsequent final medical determination results in a medical finding, determination, or opinion that the employee no longer has a detected medical condition that places the employee at increased risk of lead exposure.

The employer must remove any limitations placed on employees or end any special protective measures when a subsequent final

medical determination indicates they are no longer necessary. If the former position no longer exists, the employee is returned consistent with whatever job assignment discretion the employer would have had if no removal occurred.

WORKER PROTECTIONS AND BENEFITS

The employer must provide up to 18 months of medical removal protection (MRP) benefits each time an employee is removed from lead exposure or medically limited. As long as the position/job exists, the employer must maintain the earnings, seniority, and other employment rights and benefits as though the employee had not been removed from the job or otherwise medically limited. The employer may condition medical removal protection benefits on the employee's participation in followup medical surveillance.

If a removed employee files a worker's compensation claim or other compensation for lost wages due to a lead-related disability, the employer must continue medical removal protection benefits until the claim is resolved. However, the employer's MRP benefits obligation will be reduced by the amount that the employee receives from these sources. Also, the employer's MRP benefits obligation will be reduced by any income the employee receives from employment with another employer made possible by virtue of the employee's removal.

RECORDS REQUIREMENTS INVOLVING MEDICAL REMOVAL

In the case of medical removal, the employer's records must include:

- The worker's name and social security number,
- The date of each occasion that the worker was removed from current exposure to lead,
- The date when the worker was returned to the former job status,
- A brief explanation of how each removal was or is being accomplished, and
- A statement indicating whether the reason for the removal was an elevated blood lead level.

Recordkeeping

EMPLOYER REQUIREMENTS

The employer must maintain any employee exposure and medical records to document ongoing employee exposure, medical monitoring, and medical removal of workers. This data provides a baseline to evaluate the employee's health properly. Employees or former employees, their designated representatives, and OSHA must have access to exposure and medical records in accordance with 29 CFR 1910.1020. Rules of agency practice and procedure governing OSHA access to employee medical records are found in 29 CFR 1913.10.

EXPOSURE ASSESSMENT RECORDS

The employer must establish and maintain an accurate record of all monitoring and other data used to conduct employee exposure assessments as required by this standard and in accordance with 29 CFR 1910.1020. The exposure assessment records must include:

- The dates, number, duration, location, and results of each sample taken, including a description of the sampling procedure used to determine representative employee exposure;
- A description of the sampling and analytical methods used and evidence of their accuracy;
- The type of respiratory protection worn, if any;
- The name, social security number, and job classification of the monitored employee and all others whose exposure the measurement represents; and
- Environmental variables that could affect the measurement of employee exposure.

MEDICAL SURVEILLANCE RECORDS

The employer must maintain an accurate record for each employee subject to medical surveillance, including:

- The name, social security number, and description of the employee's duties;
- A copy of the physician's written opinions;

- The results of any airborne exposure monitoring done for the employee and provided to the physician; and

- Any employee medical complaints related to lead exposure.

  In addition, the employer must keep or ensure that the examining physician keeps the following medical records:

- A copy of the medical examination results including medical and work history;

- A description of the laboratory procedures and a copy of any guidelines used to interpret the test results; and

- A copy of the results of biological monitoring.

  The employer or physician or both must maintain medical records in accordance with 29 CFR 1910.1020.

DOCUMENTS FOR EMPLOYEES SUBJECT TO MEDICAL REMOVAL

The employer must maintain--for at least the duration of employment--an accurate record for each employee subject to medical removal, including:

- The name and social security number of the employee;

- The date on each occasion that the employee was removed from current exposure to lead and the corresponding date which the employee was returned to former job status;

- A brief explanation of how each removal was or is being accomplished; and

- A statement about each removal indicating whether the reason for removal was an elevated blood level.

EMPLOYER REQUIREMENTS RELATED TO OBJECTIVE DATA

The employer must establish and maintain an accurate record documenting the nature and relevancy of objective data relied on to assess initial employee exposure in lieu of exposure monitoring. The employer must maintain the record of objective data relied on for at least 30 years.

DOCUMENTS FOR OSHA AND NIOSH REVIEW

The employer must make all records--including exposure monitoring, objective data, medical removal, and medical records--

available upon request to affected employees, former employees, and their designated representatives and to the OSHA Assistant Secretary and the Director of the National Institute for Occupational Safety and Health (NIOSH) for examination and copying in accordance with 29 CFR 1910.1020.

WHEN CLOSING A BUSINESS

When an employer ceases to do business, the successor employer must receive and retain all required records. If no successor is available, these records must be sent to the Director of NIOSH.

Exposure Reduction and Employee Protection

The most effective way to protect workers is to minimize their exposure through engineering controls, good work practices and training, and use of personal protective clothing and equipment, including respirators, where required. The employer needs to designate a competent person capable of identifying existing and predictable lead hazards and who is authorized to take prompt corrective measures to eliminate such problems. The employer should, as needed, consult a qualified safety and health professional to develop and implement an effective worker protection program. These professionals may work independently or may be associated with an insurance carrier, trade organization, or on-site consultation program.

Engineering Controls

Engineering measures include local and general exhaust ventilation, process and equipment modification, material substitution, component replacement, and isolation or automation. Examples of recommended engineering controls that can help reduce worker exposure to lead are described as follows.

EXHAUST VENTILATION

Equip power tools used to remove lead-based paint with dust collection shrouds or other attachments so that paint is exhausted

through a high-efficiency particulate air (HEPA) vacuum system. For operations such as welding, cutting/burning, or heating, use local exhaust ventilation. Use HEPA vacuums during cleanup operations.

For abrasive blasting operations, build a containment structure that is designed to optimize the flow of clean ventilation air past the workers' breathing zones. This will help reduce the exposure to airborne lead and increase visibility. Maintain the affected area under negative pressure to reduce the chances that lead dust will contaminate areas outside the enclosure. Equip the containment structure with an adequately sized dust collector to control emissions of particulate matter into the environment.

ENCLOSURE OR ENCAPSULATION

One way to reduce the lead inhalation or ingestion hazard posed by lead-based paint is to encapsulate it with a material that bonds to the surface, such as acrylic or epoxy coating or flexible wall coverings. Another option is to enclose it using systems such as gypsum wallboard, plywood paneling, and aluminum, vinyl, or wood exterior siding. Floors coated with lead-based paint can be covered using vinyl tile or linoleum.

The building owner or other responsible person should oversee the custodial and maintenance staffs and contractors during all activities involving enclosed or encapsulated lead-based paint. This will minimize the potential for an inadvertent lead release during maintenance, renovation, or demolition.

SUBSTITUTION

Choose materials and chemicals that do not contain lead for construction projects. Among the options are:

- Use zinc-containing primers covered by an epoxy intermediate coat and polyurethane topcoat instead of lead-containing coatings.
- Substitute mobile hydraulic shears for torch cutting under certain circumstances.
- Consider surface preparation equipment such as needle guns with multiple reciprocating needles completely enclosed within an adjustable shroud, instead of abrasive blasting under certain

conditions. The shroud captures dust and debris at the cutting edge and can be equipped with a HEPA vacuum filtration with a self-drumming feature. One such commercial unit can remove lead-based paint from flat steel and concrete surfaces, outside edges, inside corners, and pipes.

- Choose chemical strippers in lieu of hand scraping with a heat gun for work on building exteriors, surfaces involving carvings or molding, or intricate iron work. Chemical removal generates less airborne lead dust. (Be aware, however, that these strippers themselves can be hazardous and that the employer must review the material safety data sheets (MSDSs) for these stripping agents to obtain information on their hazards.)

COMPONENT REPLACEMENT

Replace lead-based painted building components such as windows, doors, and trim with new components free of lead-containing paint. Another option is to remove the paint off site and then repaint the components with zinc-based paint before replacing them.

PROCESS OR EQUIPMENT MODIFICATION

When applying lead paints or other lead-containing coatings, use a brush or roller rather than a sprayer. This application method introduces little or no paint mist into the air to present a lead inhalation hazard. (Note that there is a ban on the use of lead-based paint in residential housing.)

Use non-silica-containing abrasives such as steel or iron shot/grit sand instead of sand in abrasive blasting operations when practical. The free silica portion of the dust presents a respiratory health hazard.

When appropriate for the conditions, choose blasting techniques that are less dusty than open-air abrasive blasting. These include hydro- or wet-blasting using high-pressure water with or without an abrasive or surrounding the blast nozzle with a ring of water, and vacuum blasting where a vacuum hood for material removal is positioned around the exterior of the blasting nozzle.

When using a heat gun to remove lead-based paints in residential housing units, be sure it is of the flameless electrical softener

type. Heat guns should have electronically controlled temperature settings to allow usage below 700 degrees F. Equip heat guns with various nozzles to cover all common applications and to limit the size of the heated work area.

When using abrasive blasting with a vacuum hood on exterior building surfaces, ensure that the configuration of the heads on the blasting nozzle match the configuration of the substrate so that the vacuum is effective in containing debris.

Ensure that HEPA vacuum cleaners have the appropriate attachments for use on unusual surfaces. Proper use of brushes of various sizes, crevice and angular tools, when needed, will enhance the quality of the HEPA-vacuuming process and help reduce the amount of lead dust released into the air.

ISOLATION

Although it is not feasible to enclose and ventilate some abrasive blasting operations completely, it is possible to isolate many operations to help reduce the potential for lead exposure. Isolation consists of keeping employees not involved in the blasting operations as far away from the work area as possible, reducing the risk of exposure.

Housekeeping and Personal Hygiene

Lead is a cumulative and persistent toxic substance that poses a serious health risk. A rigorous housekeeping program and the observance of basic personal hygiene practices will minimize employee exposure to lead. In addition, these two elements of the worker protection program help prevent workers from taking lead-contaminated dust out of the worksite and into their homes where it can extend the workers' exposures and potentially affect their families' health.

HOUSEKEEPING PRACTICES

An effective housekeeping program involves a regular schedule to remove accumulations of lead dust and lead-containing debris. The schedule should be adapted to exposure conditions at a particular worksite. OSHA's Lead Standard for Construction requires

employers to maintain all surfaces as free of lead contamination as practicable. Vacuuming lead dust with HEPA-filtered equipment or wetting the dust with water before sweeping are effective control measures. Compressed air may not be used to remove lead from contaminated surfaces unless a ventilation system is in place to capture the dust generated by the compressed air.

In addition, put all lead-containing debris and contaminated items accumulated for disposal into sealed, impermeable bags or other closed impermeable containers. Label bags and containers as lead-containing waste. These measures provide additional help in controlling exposure.

PERSONAL HYGIENE PRACTICES

Emphasize workers' personal hygiene such as washing their hands and face after work and before eating to minimize their exposure to lead. Provide and ensure that workers use washing facilities. Provide clean change areas and readily accessible eating areas. If possible, provide a parking area where cars will not be contaminated with lead. These measures:

- Reduce workers' exposure to lead and the likelihood that they will ingest lead,

- Ensure that the exposure does not extend beyond the worksite,

- Reduce the movement of lead from the worksite, and

- Provide added protection to employees and their families.

CHANGE AREAS

The employer must provide a clean change area for employees whose airborne exposure to lead is above the PEL. The area must be equipped with storage facilities for street clothes and a separate area with facilities for the removal and storage of lead-contaminated protective work clothing and equipment. This separation prevents cross-contamination of the employee's street and work clothing.

Employees must use a clean change area for taking off street clothes, suiting up in clean protective work clothing, donning respirators before beginning work, and dressing in street clothes after work. No lead-contaminated items should enter this area.

Work clothing must not be worn away from the jobsite. Under no circumstances should lead-contaminated work clothes be laundered at home or taken from the worksite, except to be laundered professionally or for disposal following applicable federal, state, and local regulations.

SHOWERS AND WASHING FACILITIES

When feasible, showers must be provided for use by employees whose airborne exposure to lead is above the permissible exposure limit so they can shower before leaving the worksite. Where showers are provided, employees must change out of their work clothes and shower before changing into their street clothes and leaving the worksite. If employees do not change into clean clothing before leaving the worksite, they may contaminate their homes and automobiles with lead dust, extending their exposure and exposing other members of their household to lead.

In addition, employers must provide adequate washing facilities for their workers. These facilities must be close to the worksite and furnished with water, soap, and clean towels so employees can remove lead contamination from their skin.

Contaminated water from washing facilities and showers must be disposed of in accordance with applicable local, state, or federal regulations.

PERSONAL PRACTICES

The employer must ensure that employees do not enter lunchroom facilities or eating areas with protective work clothing or equipment unless surface lead dust has been removed. HEPA vacuuming and use of a downdraft booth are examples of cleaning methods that limit the dispersion of lead dust from contaminated work clothing.

In all areas where employees are exposed to lead above the PEL, employees must observe the prohibition on the presence and con-sumption or use of food, beverages, tobacco products, and cosmetics. Employees whose airborne exposure to lead is above the PEL must wash their hands and face before eating, drinking, smoking, or applying cosmetics.

END-OF-DAY PROCEDURES

Employers must ensure that workers who are exposed to lead above the permissible exposure limit follow these procedures at the end of their workday:

- Place contaminated clothes, including work shoes and personal protective equipment to be cleaned, laundered, or disposed of, in a properly labeled closed container.
- Take a shower and wash their hair. Where showers are not provided, employees must wash their hands and face at the end of the workshift.
- Change into street clothes in clean change areas.

Protective Clothing and Equipment

EMPLOYER REQUIREMENTS

Employers must provide workers who are exposed to lead above the PEL or for whom the possibility of skin or eye irritation exists with clean, dry protective work clothing and equipment that are appropriate for the hazard. Employers must provide these items at no cost to employees. Appropriate protective work clothing and equipment used on construction sites includes:

- Coveralls or other full-body work clothing;
- Gloves, hats, and shoes or disposable shoe coverlets;
- Vented goggles or face shields with protective spectacles or goggles;
- Welding or abrasive blasting helmets; and
- Respirators.

Clean work clothing must be issued daily for employees whose exposure levels to lead are above 200 µg/m3, weekly if exposures are above the PEL but at or below 200 µg/m3 or where the possibility of skin or eye irritation exists.

HANDLING CONTAMINATED PROTECTIVE CLOTHING

Workers must not be allowed to leave the worksite wearing lead-contaminated protective clothing or equipment. This is an essential

24

step in reducing the movement of lead contamination from the workplace into the worker's home and provides added protection for employees and their families.

Disposable coveralls and separate shoe covers may be used, if appropriate, to avoid the need for laundering. Workers must remove protective clothing in change rooms provided for that purpose.

Employers must ensure that employees leave the respirator use area to wash their faces and respirator facepieces as necessary. In addition, employers may require their employees to use HEPA vacuuming, damp wiping, or another suitable cleaning method before removing a respirator to clear loose particle contamination on the respirator and at the face-mask seal.

Place contaminated clothing that is to be cleaned, laundered, or disposed of by the employer in closed containers. Label containers with the warning: "Caution: Clothing contaminated with lead. Do not remove dust by blowing or shaking. Dispose of lead-contaminated wash water in accordance with applicable local, state, or federal regulations."

Workers responsible for handling contaminated clothing, including those in laundry services or subcontractors, must be informed in writing of the potential health hazard of lead exposure. At no time shall lead be removed from protective clothing or equipment by brushing, shaking, or blowing. These actions disperse the lead into the work area.

PREVENTING HEAT STRESS

Workers wearing protective clothing, particularly in hot environments or within containment structures, can face a risk from heat stress if proper control measures are not used.

Heat stress is caused by several interacting factors, including environmental conditions, type of protective clothing worn, the work activity required and anticipated work rate, and individual employee characteristics such as age, weight, and fitness level. When heat stress is a concern, the employer should choose lighter, less insulating protective clothing over heavier clothing, as long as

it provides adequate protection. Other measures the employer can take include: discussing the possibility of heat stress and its signs and symptoms with all workers; using appropriate work/rest regimens; and providing heat stress monitoring that includes measuring employees' heart rates, body temperatures, and weight loss. Employers must provide a source of water or electrolyte drink in a non-contaminated eating and drinking area close to the work area so workers can drink often throughout the day. Workers must wash their hands and face before drinking any fluid if their airborne exposure is above the PEL.

Respiratory Protection

Although engineering and work practice controls are the primary means of protecting workers from exposure to lead, source control at construction sites sometimes is insufficient to control exposure. In these cases, airborne lead concentrations may be high or may vary widely. Respirators often must be used to supplement engineering controls and work practices to reduce worker lead exposures below the PEL. When respirators are required, employers must provide them at no cost to workers.

The standard requires that respirators be used during periods when an employee's exposure to lead exceeds the PEL, including

- Periods necessary to install or implement engineering or work practice controls, and
- Work operations for which engineering and work practice controls are insufficient to reduce employee exposures to or below the PEL.

Respirators also must be provided upon employee request. A requested respirator is included as a requirement to provide increased protection for those employees who wish to reduce their lead burden below what is required by the standard, particularly if they intend to have children in the near future. In addition, respirators must be used when performing previously indicated high exposure or "trigger" tasks, before completion of the initial assessment.

Before any employee first starts wearing a respirator in the work environment, the employer must perform a fit test. For all employees wearing negative or positive pressure tight-fitting facepiece respirators, the employer must perform either qualitative or quantitative fit tests using an OSHA-accepted fit testing protocol. In addition, employees must be fit tested whenever a different respirator facepiece is used, and at least annually thereafter.

Where daily airborne exposure to lead exceeds 50 µg/m3, affected workers must don respirators before entering the work area and should not remove them until they leave the high-exposure area or have completed a decontamination procedure. Employers must assure that the respirator issued to the employee is selected and fitted properly to ensure minimum leakage through the facepiece-to-face seal.

When respirators are required at a worksite, the employer must establish a respiratory protection program in accordance with the OSHA standard on respiratory protection, 29 CFR 1910.134. At a minimum, an acceptable respirator program for lead must include:

- Procedures for selecting respirators appropriate to the hazard;

- Fit testing procedures;

- Procedures for proper use of respirators in routine and reasonably foreseeable emergency situations, including cartridge change schedules;

- Procedures and schedules for cleaning, disinfecting, storing, inspecting, repairing, discarding, and otherwise maintaining respirators;

- Training of employees in the respiratory hazard to which they are potentially exposed during routine and emergency situations;

- Training of employees in the proper use of respirators, including putting on and removing them, any limitations of their use, and their maintenance;

- Procedures for regularly evaluating the effectiveness of the program;
- Procedures to ensure air quality when supplied air is used;
- A written program and designation of a program administrator; and
- Recordkeeping procedures.

In addition, the construction industry lead standard stipulates medical evaluations of employees required to use respirators.

If an employee has difficulty in breathing during a fit test or while using a respirator, the employer must make a medical examination available to that employee to determine whether he or she can wear a respirator safely.

SELECTING A RESPIRATOR

The employer must select the appropriate respirator from Table 1 of the lead standard, 29 CFR 1926.62(f)(3)(i). The employer must provide a powered air-purifying respirator when an employee chooses to use this respirator and it will provide the employee adequate protection. A NIOSH-certified respirator must be selected and used in compliance with the conditions of its certification. In addition, if exposure monitoring or experience indicates airborne exposures to contaminants other than lead such as silica, solvents, or polyurethane coatings, these exposures must be considered when selecting respiratory protection.

Select type CE respirators approved by NIOSH for abrasive blasting operations. Currently, there are two kinds of CE respirators with the following assigned protection factors (APFs): a continuous-flow respirator with a loose-fitting hood, APF 25; and a full facepiece supplied-air respirator operated in a positive-pressure mode, APF 2,000. (Note: OSHA recognizes Bullard Helmets, Models 77 and 88 (1995); Clemco Appollo, Models 20 and 60 (1997); and 3M Model 8100 (1998) as having APFs of 1,000.)

For any airline respirator, it is important to follow the manufacturer's instructions regarding air quality, air pressure, and inside diameter and length of hoses. Be aware that using longer hoses or smaller inside diameter hoses than the manufacturer specifies or

hoses with bends or kinks may reduce or restrict the airflow to a respirator.

Employee Information and Training

The employer must inform employees about lead hazards according to the requirement of OSHA's Hazard Communication standard for the construction industry, 29 CFR 1926.59, including-- but not limited to--the requirements for warning signs and labels, material safety data sheets (MSDSs), and employee information and training. (Refer to 29 CFR 1910.1200.)

PROGRAM REQUIREMENTS

Employers must institute an information and training program and ensure that all employees subject to exposure to lead or lead compounds at or above the action level on any day participate. Also covered under information and training are employees who may suffer skin or eye irritation from lead compounds. Initial training must be provided before the initial job assignment. Training must be repeated at least annually and, in brief summary, must include:

- The content of the OSHA lead standard and its appendices;
- The specific nature of operations that could lead to lead exposure above the action level;
- The purpose, proper selection, fit, use, and limitations of respirators;
- The purpose and a description of the medical surveillance program, and the medical removal protection program;
- Information concerning the adverse health effects associated with excessive lead exposure;
- The engineering and work practice controls associated with employees' job assignments;
- The contents of any lead-related compliance plan in effect;
- Instructions to employees that chelating agents must not be used routinely to remove lead from their bodies and when necessary only under medical supervision and at the direction of a licensed physician; and

- The right to access records under "Access to Employee Exposure and Medical Records," 29 CFR 1910.1020.

All materials relating to the training program and a copy of the standard and its appendices must be made readily available to all affected employees.

WARNING SIGNS

Employers are required to post these warning signs in each work area where employee exposure to lead is above the PEL:

- WARNING
- LEAD WORK AREA
- POISON
- NO SMOKING OR EATING

All signs must be well lit and kept clean so that they are easily visible. Statements that contradict or detract from the signs' meaning are prohibited. Signs required by other statutes, regulations, or ordinances, however, may be posted in addition to, or in combination with, this sign.

OSHA Assistance

OSHA can provide extensive help through a variety of programs, including technical assistance about effective safety and health programs, state plans, workplace consultations, voluntary protection programs, strategic partnerships, training and education, and more. An overall commitment to workplace safety and health can add value to your business, to your workplace and to your life.

SAFETY AND HEALTH PROGRAM MANAGEMENT GUIDELINES

Effective management of employee safety and health protection is a decisive factor in reducing the extent and severity of work-related injuries and illnesses and their related costs. In fact, an effective safety and health program forms the basis of good employee protection can save time and money, increase productivity, reduce employee injuries, illnesses and related workers' compensation costs.

To assist employers and employees in developing effective safety and health programs, OSHA published recommended Safety and Health Program Management Guidelines (54 Federal Register (16): 3904-3916, January 26, 1989). These voluntary guidelines apply to all places of employment covered by OSHA.

The guidelines identify four general elements critical to the development of a successful safety and health management system:

- Management leadership and employee involvement,
- Worksite analysis,
- Hazard prevention and control, and
- Safety and health training.

The guidelines recommend specific actions, under each of these general elements, to achieve an effective safety and health program. The Federal Register notice is available online at www.osha.gov.

STATE PROGRAMS

The Occupational Safety and Health Act of 1970 (OSH Act) encourages states to develop and operate their own job safety and health plans. OSHA approves and monitors these plans. Twenty-four states, Puerto Rico, and the Virgin Islands currently operate approved state plans: 22 cover both private and public (state and local government) employment; Connecticut, New Jersey, New York and the Virgin Islands cover the public sector only. States and territories with their own OSHA-approved occupational safety and health plans must adopt standards identical to, or at least as effective as, the Federal OSHA standards.

CONSULTATION SERVICES

Consultation assistance is available on request to employers who want help in establishing and maintaining a safe and healthful workplace. Largely funded by OSHA, the service is provided at no cost to the employer. Primarily developed for smaller employers with more hazardous operations, the consultation service is delivered by state governments employing professional safety and health

consultants. Comprehensive assistance includes an appraisal of all mechanical systems, work practices and occupational safety and health hazards of the workplace and all aspects of the employer's present job safety and health program. In addition, the service offers assistance to employers in developing and implementing an effective safety and health program. No penalties are proposed or citations issued for hazards identified by the consultant. OSHA provides consultation assistance to the employer with the assurance that his or her name and firm and any information about the workplace will not be routinely reported to OSHA enforcement staff.

Under the consultation program, certain exemplary employers may request participation in OSHA's Safety and Health Achievement Recognition Program (SHARP). Eligibility for participation in SHARP includes receiving a comprehensive consultation visit, demonstrating exemplary achievements in workplace safety and health by abating all identified hazards, and developing an excellent safety and health program.

Employers accepted into SHARP may receive an exemption from programmed inspections (not complaint or accident investigation inspections) for a period of one year. For more information concerning consultation assistance, see the OSHA website at www.osha.gov.

VOLUNTARY PROTECTION PROGRAMS

Voluntary Protection Programs and on-site consultation services, when coupled with an effective enforcement program, expand employee protection to help meet the goals of the OSH Act. The VPPs motivate others to achieve excellent safety and health results in the same outstanding way as they establish a cooperative relationship between employers, employees and OSHA.

For additional information on VPP and how to apply, contact the OSHA regional offices listed at the end of this publication.

STRATEGIC PARTNERSHIP PROGRAM

OSHA's Strategic Partnership Program, the newest member of OSHA's cooperative programs, helps encourage, assist and recognize the efforts of partners to eliminate serious workplace

hazards and achieve a high level of employee safety and health. Whereas OSHA's Consultation Program and VPP entail one-on-one relationships between OSHA and individual worksites, most strategic partnerships seek to have a broader impact by building cooperative relationships with groups of employers and employees. These partnerships are voluntary, cooperative relationships between OSHA, employers, employee representatives and others (e.g., trade unions, trade and professional associations, universities and other government agencies).

For more information on this and other cooperative programs, contact your nearest OSHA office, or visit OSHA's website at www.osha.gov.

ALLIANCE PROGRAM

Through the Alliance Program, OSHA works with groups committed to safety and health, including businesses, trade or professional organizations, unions and educational institutions, to leverage resources and expertise to develop compliance assistance tools and resources and share information with employers and employees to help prevent injuries, illnesses and fatalities in the workplace.

Alliance program agreements have been established with a wide variety of industries including meat, apparel, poultry, steel, plastics, maritime, printing, chemical, construction, paper and telecommunications. These agreements are addressing many safety and health hazards and at-risk audiences, including silica, fall protection, amputations, immigrant workers, youth and small businesses. By meeting the goals of the Alliance Program agreements (training and education, outreach and communication, and promoting the national dialogue on workplace safety and health), OSHA and the Alliance Program participants are developing and disseminating compliance assistance information and resources for employers and employees such as electronic assistance tools, fact sheets, toolbox talks, and training programs.

OSHA TRAINING AND EDUCATION

OSHA area offices offer a variety of information services, such

www.osha.gov

as compliance assistance, technical advice, publications, audiovisual aids and speakers for special engagements. OSHA's Training Institute in Arlington Heights, IL, provides basic and advanced courses in safety and health for Federal and state compliance officers, state consultants, Federal agency personnel, and private sector employers, employees and their representatives.

The OSHA Training Institute also has established OSHA Training Institute Education Centers to address the increased demand for its courses from the private sector and from other federal agencies. These centers include colleges, universities and nonprofit training organizations that have been selected after a competition for participation in the program.

OSHA also provides funds to nonprofit organizations, through grants, to conduct workplace training and education in subjects where OSHA believes there is a lack of workplace training. Grants are awarded annually. Grant recipients are expected to contribute 20 percent of the total grant cost.

For more information on grants, training and education, contact the OSHA Training Institute, Directorate of Training and Education, 2020 South Arlington Heights Road, Arlington Heights, IL 60005, (847) 297-4810 or see Training on OSHA's website at www.osha.gov. For further information on any OSHA program, contact your nearest OSHA regional office listed at the end of this publication.

INFORMATION AVAILABLE ELECTRONICALLY

OSHA has a variety of materials and tools available on its website at www.osha.gov. These include electronic compliance assistance tools, such as *Safety and Health Topics Pages, eTools, Expert Advisors;* regulations, directives, publications and videos; and other information for employers and employees. OSHA's software programs and compliance assistance tools walk you through challenging safety and health issues and common problems to find the best solutions for your workplace.

A wide variety of OSHA materials, including standards, interpretations, directives, and more can be purchased on CD-ROM from the U.S. Government Printing Office, Superintendent of Documents, toll-free phone (866) 512-1800.

34

OSHA has an extensive publications program. For a listing of free or sales items, visit OSHA's website at www.osha.gov or contact the OSHA Publications Office, U.S. Department of Labor, 200 Constitution Avenue, NW, N-3101, Washington, DC 20210. Telephone (202) 693-1888 or fax to (202) 693-2498.

To report an emergency, file a complaint or seek OSHA advice, assistance or products, call (800) 321-OSHA or contact your nearest OSHA regional or area office listed at the end of this publication. The teletypewriter (TTY) number is (877) 889-5627.

Written correspondence can be mailed to the nearest OSHA Regional or Area Office listed at the end of this publication or to OSHA's national office at: U.S. Department of Labor, Occupational Safety and Health Administration, 200 Constitution Avenue, N.W., Washington, DC 20210.

By visiting OSHA's website at www.osha.gov, you can also:

- File a complaint online,
- Submit general inquiries about workplace safety and health electronically, and
- Find more information about OSHA and occupational safety and health.

OSHA Regional Offices

Region I
(CT,* ME, MA, NH, RI, VT*)
JFK Federal Building, Room E340
Boston, MA 02203
(617) 565-9860

Region II
(NJ,* NY,* PR,* VI*)
201 Varick Street, Room 670
New York, NY 10014
(212) 337-2378

Region III
(DE, DC, MD,* PA,* VA,* WV)
The Curtis Center
170 S. Independence Mall West
Suite 740 West
Philadelphia, PA 19106-3309
(215) 861-4900

Region IV
(AL, FL, GA, KY,* MS, NC,* SC,* TN*)
61 Forsyth Street, SW, Room 6T50
Atlanta, GA 30303
(404) 562-2300

Region V
(IL, IN,* MI,* MN,* OH, WI)
230 South Dearborn Street, Room 3244
Chicago, IL 60604
(312) 353-2220

Region VI
(AR, LA, NM,* OK, TX)
525 Griffin Street, Room 602
Dallas, TX 75202
(972) 850-4145

Region VII
(IA,* KS, MO, NE)
Two Pershing Square
2300 Main Street, Suite 1010
Kansas City, MO 64108-2416
(816) 283-8745

Region VIII
(CO, MT, ND, SD, UT,* WY*)
1999 Broadway, Suite 1690
PO Box 46550
Denver, CO 80202-5716
(720) 264-6550

Region IX
(AZ,* CA,* HI, NV,* and American Samoa, Guam
and the Northern Mariana Islands)
90 7th Street, Suite 18-100
San Francisco, CA 94103
(415) 625-2547

Region X
(AK,* ID, OR,* WA*)
1111 Third Avenue, Suite 715
Seattle, WA 98101-3212
(206) 553-5930

* These states and territories operate their own OSHA-approved job safety and health programs and cover state and local government employees as well as private sector employees. The Connecticut, New Jersey, New York and Virgin Islands plans cover public employees only. States with approved programs must have standards that are identical to, or at least as effective as, the Federal OSHA standards.

Note: To get contact information for OSHA Area Offices, OSHA-approved State Plans and OSHA Consultation Projects, please visit us online at www.osha.gov or call us at 1-800-321-OSHA.